Adlestrop Remembered

Adlestrop

Yes. I remember Adlestrop –
The name, because one afternoon
Of heat the express-train drew up there
Unwontedly. It was late June.

The steam hissed. Someone cleared his throat.
No one left and no one came
On the bare platform. What I saw
Was Adlestrop – only the name

And willows, willow-herb, and grass,
And meadowsweet, and haycocks dry,
No whit less still and lonely fair
Than the high cloudlets in the sky.

And for that minute a blackbird sang
Close by, and round him, mistier,
Farther and farther, all the birds
Of Oxfordshire and Gloucestershire.

Edward Thomas

ADLESTROP REMEMBERED

A Poetry Anthology
from the Centenary Competition

Edited by Victoria Huxley

All proceeds from the sale of this book go to
church funds for St Mary Magdalene, Adlestrop

 Windrush

First published in Great Britain in 2014 by
WINDRUSH PUBLISHING SERVICES
Windrush House, 12 Main Street
Adlestrop, Moreton in Marsh
Gloucestershire GL56 0UN
01608 659328

British Library Cataloguing in Publication Data

A catalogue record of this book is available from the British Library

ISBN 978 0 9575150 3 1

Cover, design and typesetting by Geoffrey Smith, Windrush Publishing Services

Line drawings by Pam Crook

Printed and bound in the UK by imprintdigital.com

www.adlestroppoem.wordpress.com

Contents

Contents

Foreword

Edward Thomas was an obsessive filler-up of notebooks. In prose (*In Pursuit of Spring*) he chides himself for this: most of what he notes turns out to be useless.

On 24 June 1914 he went by train across country to visit his friend Robert Frost in Dymock (Herefordshire). For some reason the train stopped briefly ('unwontedly') at a platform with the sign 'Adlestrop'.

A few months later, in 1915, when he had begun to write poems (having enlisted in the Army although over-age; later he was posted to France, from which he did not return) he came across the word 'Adlestrop' – in a notebook, of course – and wrote 16 lines, which begin doubtfully: 'Yes, I remember Adlestrop – / The name ...' as though he could remember nothing else, for the moment. This is hardly surprising, for not much else happened during that brief halt, except ordinary life: 'Someone cleared his throat. / No one left and no one came ...' Then a blackbird sang and its singing seemed to multiply until the air was filled with it, and 'Farther and farther, all the birds / Of Oxfordshire and Gloucestershire.' After the mundane comes a hint of the universal.

This year, 2014, to honour the centenary, Victoria Huxley, who lives in Adlestrop, decided to run a poetry competition, the winner to be announced at an event by the Friends of the Dymock Poets. Poems were to be based on Thomas's 'Adlestrop', to discover what people made of it now, because over the decades it has become widely popular.

The result was astonishing: nearly two hundred entries, nearly all of them evidence that the writers had somehow understood the poem, and in different ways. Poems can sometimes touch a nerve, indeed do not need to be 'understood' at all, in the ordinary sense, but can be felt, beyond explanation. Those brief moments of silence, perhaps bewilderment, a sense of confinement suddenly opening out into a wider, more thrilling world, had been felt, and in that way understood, by entry after entry. Maybe they all deserved a prize. Perhaps their prize was their own poem.

P.J.Kavanagh
September 2014

Introduction

The twenty-fourth of June 2014 was an important date for the village of Adlestrop. It was on that Midsummer's Day, exactly a hundred years ago, that Edward Thomas made his train journey from London to Ledbury. Accompanied by his wife, Helen, he was going to meet his friends who would later come to be known as the 'Dymock Poets' and on the way the steam train paused at Adlestrop station.

Later, in January 1915, he distilled the jottings he had made in his notebook into the poem 'Adlestrop'. Six months after Edward Thomas' death at the Battle of Arras on Easter Monday, 9 April 1917, the poem was published together with 63 other poems. Since then the poem has become almost a talisman for a memory of an English country idyll. A vision lost after the First World War which was declared just over a month after that train journey.

To celebrate the poem I decided to organise a Poetry Competition to raise money for the Fabric Fund of the parish church in the village. In this I was greatly helped by fellow villagers, John Gillett, Ernest Johnson and Gordon Harris as well as Anne Harvey, the author of *Adlestrop Revisited*. Anne Harvey is also a leading light in the poetry world and had run many poetry competitions and edited several anthologies and helped me greatly all along the way. She introduced me to the distinguished poet, P.J. Kavanagh, who was the ideal judge of the competition entries — not only does he live in Gloucestershire, — but he is extremely knowledgeable about Edward Thomas, has written poems about him and introduced collections of his prose.

At first there were few poems but as the weeks went on, more and more came through my letter box and every day was a feast of discovery and delighted surprise that so many poets (most never published before) should be inspired to write for the competition. The condition of entry was simple: to write a poem the same length as the original (16 lines) and for it to have been inspired by the

Introduction

original. In the end 197 entries were received from all over Britain and the world. I was overwhelmed by their diversity and high quality.

———•———

The anniversary was a wonderful day in Adlestrop — the weather was hot and perfect, blue sky with some high clouds, and the Cotswolds and the village looked beautiful. In the Village Hall an audience of almost 100 people from the Friends of the Dymock Poets met for a day of readings, talks and discussions about the poem, which would culminate with the announcement of the winner of the Adlestrop Centenary Poetry Competition. This was not all: a commemorative train ran from Oxford to Moreton in Marsh, stopping in a field not far from the original station, where a new station sign had been erected, specially commissioned by Ralph Price and Gordon Harris. Young Victoria Edwards, who lives in Adlestrop, read her own poem about Edward Thomas to all the passengers, and then 'Adlestrop' was read aloud by Lord Faulkner, president of the Cotswold Line Promotion Group, after a short talk about the poet. In Adlestrop itself a group of visitors and villagers saw the stationary train from a vantage point outside Adlestrop House and simultaneously heard the poem recited by villager, Stuart Dewar. It was a memorable moment.

Lots of unexpected people came to the village that day, including the Diatonics, a choir from Warwick, who had set the poem to music and sang in the village hall and at other places to the many visitors who looked for the station, the train and the iconic bench. Another welcome surprise was the stand made by letter carver, Paul Thomas, who had recreated the original Adlestrop Station nameboard and platform bench. Having won five gold stars at the Chelsea Flower Show, Paul rebuilt it outside the Village Hall. All in all it was an exhilarating occasion and one which I feel would have amazed Edward Thomas.

At 4 o'clock, the judge of the competition, P.J. Kavanagh, read David Sutton's winning poem to a rapt audience, and presented him with his £400 prize cheque and a calligraphy scroll of his poem. He said:

'What I liked about the winner was a tactile memory. Steam train, being included in the steam (the writer I mean), the slats of the tarry footbridge that "tingled underfoot", the cloud of steam (and the emergence from it), suggested to me the confusion of the war Thomas was about to go into and not emerge from, but the children in the steam-cloud did emerge, and so, last phrase of the poem, "the song went on".

'As for the standard of the entries, nearly two hundred, it seemed to me surprisingly good, considering the conditions of the competition, 16 lines, 'Adlestrop' etc. I was very impressed. This poem, to me, stood out, but the choice of runners-up was difficult, there were so many to choose from.'

⋅—◆—⋅

The winning poet, David Sutton, lives in South Oxfordshire and has published eight books of poetry, the last being *No Through Road* published by the Greenwich Exchange. He was inspired to write the poem after first visiting Adlestrop in 1961:

'I remember passing through Adlestrop on a cycling tour in the summer of 1961, when I was seventeen, and stopping on the railway bridge to take a drink from my water-bottle. A passer-by told me that a good poem had been written about the place. At that time I had never heard of Edward Thomas, and it was hard to see what

Introduction

there was about this very quiet scene to make a poem out of, but when I got back I managed to find 'Adlestrop' in an anthology, and that was the start of a lifelong devotion to the poet of all poets who spoke to me most clearly about the things that I loved in a language that I instinctively understood.

'When I came to write my poem for the competition, this memory became fused with an earlier memory from my childhood: there was a railway at the bottom of the road where I lived, and a narrow bridge (long since replaced by a more modern structure) where we children (free to roam in those days) would stand to watch the trains go by beneath. So the poem is a little about me, but much more, I like to think, about the poet in that far off summer, and the heritage he left us, that if anything speaks to us ever more clearly with the passing of time: the years go by, but the song goes on.'

I would like to thank the following (in no particular order) for all their help in putting the competition and book together, making generous donations of either time or money: Geoffrey Smith, Anne Harvey, John Gillett, Gordon Harris, John Ellis, Ralph and Angela Price, Gordon Ottewell, Jeff Cooper, Kate Kavanagh, P.J. Kavanagh, Ernest Johnson, Brian Clayton, John Monks, Heather Cobby, Jinnie Holt, Candia McKormack, Pamela Tomlinson, Mark Smalley and Pam Crook for her line drawings.

But most of all I would like to thank all the poets who entered the competition for their inspired poems and their tributes to Edward Thomas and the village of Adlestrop.

Victoria Huxley
Adlestrop, 2014

The Winning Poem

'One afternoon of heat the express-train…'

To stand on the railway bridge – that was the dare
When we were children, while the last steam trains
Thundered beneath us, blotting out our world
With acrid gritty grey, and tarry slats
Tingled underfoot. When we came down
Pleased with our childish valour, earth and sky
Unclouding seemed the sweeter: I rejoiced
At sunlight on my face, the song of birds.

Now when I read your poem this comes back
But what I see is not myself but you,
The watchful traveller, nerving yourself
Soon to a more dreadful dare, but then
Getting it down at last, before your world
Was blotted out forever: haycocks, clouds,
While round you, near and far, and farther yet
Than you could ever know, the song went on.

DAVID SUTTON

Finalist

Playing Trains

i m Maurice Turner

If Maurice didn't come in for his tea, he'd be
down at the station playing signalman
or station master. Blowing the guard's whistle.
I'd send Fred, my eldest, to bring him home.

Later, both left by train, my lads. So smart,
khaki. I couldn't bear to see them off – kissed
them goodbye in the kitchen, at home.
From the back, they looked identical.

I was in the kitchen washing the windows
when the telegram came: Wounded gravely.
That was Monday. Then Friday: It is my
sad duty. I had to write to Fred.

Maurice comes home today. He'd have loved
to see it - even Adlestrop band, of sorts.
The Station Master and the signalman,
waiting for his train. An unscheduled stop.

VANESSA GEBBIE

18 year old Maurice Turner, Driver 199235 Royal Field Artillery, died 20.2.1917 at Brighton Military Hospital and is buried in the churchyard of St Mary Magdalene, Adlestrop. His brother Frederick, Pte 51014 9th Cheshire Regt, died 19.7.1917, aged 31. He is buried in Oosttaverne Cemetery, Belgium.

Finalist

A Premonition

Who was it that cleared his throat
To what end? With something to say
Before he thought the better of it
And settled back in the only way

Of being a ghost? Let birdsong,
Risen above all incidental sounds,
Leave its crescendo with the living
As music is a wordlessness that mends.

Besides, what would be broken
But his heart by hearing said
All he could utter of those men,
His travelling companions, the dead

He now belonged with? Life
Best left for those with time to dream
Their onward journey, and grief
A bare platform, a hiss of steam.

JOHN MOLE

Finalist

Medlow Bath

Yes. I remember Medlow Bath —
The name, because one clear, cold afternoon
The express-train drew up there
Unwontedly. It was late June.

The steam hissed. Some one cleared his throat.
No one left and no one came
On the bare platform. What I saw
Was Medlow Bath — only the name.

And pine trees, eucalypts, and grass,
And banksias, and tussocks dry,
No whit less still and lonely fair
Than the high cloudlets in the sky.

And for that minute a currawong sang
Close by, and round him, without fail,
Farther and farther, all the currawongs
From Hazelbrook to Hartley Vale.

DENIS RICE

I often imagine that Edward Thomas survived the battlefields of France and in 1920 visited Australia where he travelled by fast train from Sydney along the Western line over the Blue Mountains to the historic town of Bathurst. I further imagine that the train he was on made an unaccustomed stop at Medlow Bath, the first station west of Katoomba.

Finalist

Adlestrop Unwound

I've quite forgotten Adlestrop,
Upper Slaughter, Lower Slaughter,
Foggy Bottom, Devil's Drop,
Faintley-Furtive-in-the-Water,

Squeezegut Alley, Nettlefold,
Bogshole, Chicksands, Chickenshit,
Little-Piddle-on-the-Wold,
Porlock, Warlock, Witch's Tit,

Stinking Bishop. I don't think
I'm happy with a lot of those.
God, I need another drink!
Plumstead, Bumstead, Parson's Nose?

The Leith Police dismisseth us.
Is Leith a place? And where if so?
Carcinoma, Platypus,
Steeple Bastard? I don't know.

JOHN WHITWORTH

Finalist

Remembering 'Adlestrop'

I first encountered 'Adlestrop'
when just a youngster; squeaky, keen,
I heard the word, poetic nerd,
had no idea what it might mean.

The crashing warfare of our youth;
my brother raiding refuge, den,
left no ceasefire to contemplate
my trenchant heartsongs then.

There was a moment it was used –
all sibilant steam and plosive pop –
by Mum - her pun on teenage rage
and tantrum: Adolescent Strop.

Late now; beyond the years of green
and golden hopes since faded, gone,
faint echo of his untamed song,
like 'Adlestrop', still lingers on.

ALEXANDRA DAVIS

Change at Adlestrop

Those birds sang fiercely what is true.
Whirling; commanding us to stop,
To hearken to their hoard of song –
Yes, I remember Adlestrop.

Those gone are those who had to go.
Our light tread makes our path wear smooth.
We are all earth's, as all are sky's;
Our ghosts the aspens mark and soothe.

The consummation I desired –
To lie in earth; say 'it is over' –
Was Hamlet's, and became my song,
A sweeter prize than any lover.

A century of dung-filled years from this,
Historians will find, perchance,
What I have left – my secret code –
My seeking of a grave in France.

GAVIN SMITHERS

Tomato Sandwiches

The knife slides through the warm bread
Plunging me back to teenage summer heat
When Grandma, dying, asked for sandwiches
I knew she would but could not eat.

Sweet scent of tomato, sharp salt and pepper,
Sliced and diced, soft butter spread
On bread cut, crustless, less than child size,
A tender recipe, an offering to the not quite dead.

She thanked me with her eyes, she tried to eat,
The tiny morsels pushed around the plate
Too much for her. She slept at last and, watching her,
With youthful appetite and absent mind, I ate.

I watched her breathe, uneasy at the laboured breath,
I viewed the desperate landscape of the old and ill
I understood her kindness in the face of death
And learned that love and tenderness endure there still.

RUTH OINN

2014

The years have turned. Again it's June,
The peaceful village seems the same
With fields and trees lit up by sun.
Yet on a bench the station's name.

The hedgerows neat and newly trimmed,
Verges bedecked with flowers still.
The birds are sadly fewer now,
But yet is heard the blackbird's trill.

Thomas and Austen, writers both,
Their ghosts may roam the quiet lane.
Cut down too soon like country elms,
They feel no longer wind nor rain.

Now in the Shires, on country lines
The passing trains no longer stop.
In sweet sleep may the poet rest,
Remembered still in Adlestrop.

PAULINE NICHOLLS

Adlestrop

Curse forsaken Adlestrop
where no girls live, no band tours stop.
May no good come to Adlestrop.
May pests infest the crop
that fills the fields of Adlestrop,
and may the bell that hangs atop
St Mary's Church in Adlestrop
ring tonelessly. By the village shop
I'll howl my hate for Adlestrop,
    And I won't stop
until each man in Adlestrop,
each woman and child, is fit to drop.
You who speak of Adlestrop
as a charming place for the train to stop,
try growing up in Adlestrop.
Try that. You want to swap?

MATTHEW SPERLING

Learning By Heart, Unwontedly

Yes. I remember Adlestrop – the books
we read it in. The touch
of years of fingertips. Last week,
last term of such an endless, such

a golden-blue July. Fifteen.
We thought we knew it all. We paused
reluctantly, poised at the cusp.
Was it the willow-herb which caused

a stiller sense to waft into
the room? Pink drifts in misty sun;
the scent of candyflossy cloves...
We were absorbed – spellbound – undone.

And for that minute, no bells rang.
We weren't in English, hating
poetry, and longing to be done.
We were at Adlestrop. Waiting.

CHARITY NOVICK

End of the Line. 1917

'It's Mr Thomas, isn't it sir?
You'll not remember, but you
instructed us in the mysteries
of mapping, back when ... and sorry

we meet like this, amid so many;
must have laid on extra coaches,
and all one class, as you might say,
all in it together for the night.

Me? Yes, a railwayman sir –
had a lovely little station then.
Well, manner of speaking – just
a porter, but apprenticed, you know ...

They'll set us down soon – hard to tell
where you are in all this blasted waste ...
Dark, sir, not even a glimmer –
but it's over, isn't it – the worst?'

CHRIS WATERS

V.E. Day

I shall always remember the tenth day of May,
After six weary years it was V.E. Day,
The bunting was flying
The crowd were all crying
 'Welcome Home' to our men
Now returning, and then
A paean of church bells rang out in the air
With their jubilant message as if to declare
'It's all over' no air-raids and sirens to fear
But a glorious reunion with those we hold dear.
Though a certain misgiving it has to be said
Was niggling away in a five year old head,
Would the man in the photograph, previously not met
Be the fun-loving father so dreamed of , and yet
It was hard to accept that two would be three
After five selfish years of just Mummy and me.
Such doubts were unfounded, suffice it to say
That no date holds such joy as the tenth day of May.

SALLY NELSON

Adlestrop 21st century

Hi there,
Look, I'm going to be late
'Unscheduled stop'
Near Adlestrop I think
You know, the poetry place.
How long?
No idea. No signs, no guard
No one about to sort it out.
The noise?
Just 50 chaps phoning their wives.
Supper?
Did you say Vichysoisse?
At least it's cold.
I'll text you from the station
See you,

Whenever.

AUDREY F. TIMPSON

Edward Thomas

Yes, I remember Edward.
Tall, athletic, grey melancholy eyes
betraying his beautiful face. And his hands,
large and strong, sensitive in disguise.

He wrote of clouds and landscape,
named wild flowers. We talked of Shelley.
Once he sent me a thrush's egg, freckled blue
and we were happy in 'Love's Philosophy'.

When dark times came he often fled
but letters kept us close. Wounding words
forgotten, salved with love and shared delight
in the sky and the trees and the birds.

The last time I saw Edward, he spoke,
knowing it was a journey we could not rewind,
'Remember, all is well between us forever and ever'.
The shell that stopped his heart broke mine.

Helen L. Storey

Remembering Adlestrop

One hundred years on, near Adlestrop,
the air in June here rises hot,
and whispered birdsong echoes still
to proud men gone, but not forgot.

The village, huddled around its church,
recalls in its memorials and prayer
those who lived here, those who stopped here,
pausing on the way to their dying. Over there.

For those hundred years the mist and drip of morning rains
have softened the limestone hills, nurtured fields of wheat and oats,
pinned the medals of one hundred golden harvests
upon the sky's one hundred coats.

Here on well-worn rails the country's young,
each with his thoughts, his tin hat, his pack,
wondered at their own leaving, saw and heard the landscape's
promise:
Go, be safe, we won't forget. But too few came back.

CHRISTOPHER M. EARLE

Cheltenham Railway Station

'and for that minute a blackbird sang...' Edward Thomas

The carriages drag to a stop. Just a place on the line
for onward passengers, but my home station.
I manoeuvre myself and my luggage down from the train
into the winter evening, and pause a moment,
trying to believe I am really here again.

And now of course the wind, and a chilly drizzle –
raw homecoming. Head down, I begin hauling
my bag up the ramp at the back of the platform,
hunched against the rain relentlessly falling.
But there's something else: an outburst of birdsong
right at my ear, in that unkempt alley, spilling

from the bushes, and stronger all the time
as I look for the source. There, on a wind-whipped twig,
a robin holds tight, pouring out a psalm
of tumbling alleluias in the rain,
close by the pathway; singing me home.

CHRISTINE WHITTEMORE

Adlestrop

Adlestrop was the place you stopped,
the station where the blackbird sang,
where you waited in the heat of June
expectantly – let the time hang.

You listened to the hiss of steam,
held that moment in a trance,
and caught the note of one lone thrush,
the sound you seldom heard in France.

And someone coughed but no one came
as you watched the white, high-tiered cloud,
saw willows, willow-herb and grass.
No hint of whiz-bangs or men cowed.

You did not dream of trenches then,
of the guns which would never stop,
but held your country in your arms,
that summer's day at Adlestrop.

Denise Bennett

I am sorry Mr Thomas

I am sorry, Mr Thomas,
You only saw the name,
That day you came to Adlestrop
And never left the train.

Further from the platform
There was plenty to delight
In a village full of treasures
Where Jane Austen came to write.

You missed the church, the woods, the fields
The blossom and the brook,
The path, up high, where all around
The view is worth a look.

The locals would have welcomed you
On your exploratory endeavour,
And there is no doubt, if you'd got out,
You might have stayed for ever!

TANSY CHALLIS

After Adlestrop

They held fast through the second war
and beyond, those havens of ours.
Swanbourne served our school.

You hurried across, line level,
or slithered down the bank
to place coins on the rails.

The station master's garden,
with picture-book hollyhocks,
was a taste of Toytown,

while on our side a spinney,
dark, overgrown,
offered wild white raspberries.

On dentist jaunts to Oxford
we called at Winslow, Claydon,
Verney Junction, Marsh Gibbon, Bicester
and Islip. Adlestrops all.

RUTH MARDEN

Chassignolles

Yes, I remember 'Adlestrop' –
The poem, since one afternoon
My friends' old man pulled out his pocket-book
Of poets like Siegfried Sassoon.

The kettle hissed. He paused to clear his throat,
Then read to us from it – read 'Adlestrop' in it,
Just the three of us, glad
To stop there for that minute.

In that old French kitchen where we broke baguettes
On a stout wooden table sat on a stone floor;
The whole house still musty from pungent wild mushrooms
Brought in from the woods then put back out the door,

His voice caught as he read to us.
And the blackbird's song had travelled now
Through those other birds and Thomas, across the Channel and
    the years
To a charming room in the Auvergne. To his mouth. To our ears.

WES WHITE

Centenary Stop

We come back now and find your sign
detached from when that afternoon
a train stopped and a blackbird sang –
and all your journeys in between

pause in a solitude of sound.
We hear your voice, pure as a thrush,
live in the wind, in wet, in bright,
stayed in your calm attentiveness

to chip of flint and marguerite.
Your air is word as on the road
we too encounter those you meet
and learn the seasons of your mood.

The long echo of a shell
fades in these fields. We are held up
on stopping by this platform bench
once somewhere else. Yes. Adlestrop.

ANN ALLEN

Whitehill

It has taken a long time to bring me
to this grey February
with its raw wind and no warmth
to walk in lines in feeble light
high above the river
where opposite, beeches sweep down
to follow the grain of the slanting hill
and under the hedge
the ground cracks alarmingly
and moss curls over your faded name.
A cluster of daffodils pierces the earth
and I am carried to Formby,
a night in the balmy pinewoods
snug in the dunes with Kit-Kats and opened
bottles of lager from the pub,
watching the shipping lanes, the lights disappear.

Virginia Astley

After Adlestrop

What was the next station ?
What was he thinking?
Worcester, America,
decision, escaping?

Longing for wildness
exploring, surprise –
new words, new senses,
granted release

from that handful of English earth
he said he'd fight for –
from that peace he'd devoured
and did all for ?

Those clouds, those birds, that emptiness
free from time or decision
like the second of airlessness
before the explosion.

CATHERINE WARD

Waiting Room

With time came the curious like cats after warmth
Till piece by piece it was taken away, track,
Platform, all save the name's dry husk
Of a golden age, parched brown, that lasted

As long as a cough, a third of a page.
Turn two by mistake and in a hurry
And you'd miss it. But then so much
Is unmeant. A train pauses, a step beyond

Impatience from a world of time
Wasted, to be gazed at with a cow's gaze;
Where a song comes from a single note,
A flood from a single drop of rain,

A desert from a single grain of sand,
As a train comes to wait
Forever for the cough to cease,
Birdsong dusty in the throat.

JEFFREY TURNER

Single from Adlestrop

No, I've forgotten Adlestrop,
forgot every letter of your name
so pronounced, it hit me
like an express train. You were gone.

You drew up your ultimatum
I cleared my throat. You left
and no one came. Just this bare platform
for my heartache, you left me just the same.

Willows wept for me, and grass
in meadows sweet, waved goodbye;
tears, just raindrops passing,
doubts to cloud my eye;

a minute's silence rang
louder than a blackbird ever sang.
Steep would be my learning
you would not be returning

Isabel White

Edwardian Legacy

There is no doubting Thomas endures –
That intimate stranger haloed in the steam,
Taut between dappled June-tide warmth
And Flanders rutted spikes of death.

The drowsy sibilance of a country halt,
Expressed, beached and sheltered now,
Syncopates the century's song,
Enriching Adlestrop far beyond the name.

The stillness of serendipity whispers wide.
Shuttered hedgerows shade the village far,
While willows bend to hold the sky aloft
Weeping at the fallen poet's epitaph.

The blackbird's liquid descant of defiance
Challenges the linearity of tune,
Cleaving closer yet closer to a train of thought
That immortalised one Cotswold afternoon.

Nigel H. Williams

Remembering Adlestrop

Yes. I remember. It was late June and hot.
The train pulled up slowly with a hiss and a pant.
A man rustled his newspaper. Nobody stood
at the doors to get out. No one got on.

There was a platform bereft of greetings,
farewell kisses. No luggage strewn.
No children shouting, jumping up and down,
or peak-capped man in uniform. I saw no name.

Dust swirled slowly in a sullen breeze, vinca
trailing over parched earth had lost its gloss.
I heard no bird. Maybe all the lanes were empty,
cottages deserted. No one ever arrived or left.

I looked across at you. And we two, strangers,
mouthed together the word Adlestrop and smiled.
And in that minute, surely, a blackbird sang
and all the birds of Monmouthshire joined in.

CHRIS RAETSCHUS

Line

To satisfy a long held wish
one afternoon I took the road
across the bridge where trains still run
beside the timeless Evenlode.

Mine was no random halt. I knew
why I had come and what I came
to see but I was strangely moved
to read the sign with its bold name.

A March breeze ruffled early spring
and warm breath misted in the chill,
while the clear sound of blackbird song
pierced the quietness of the hill

as if no time had passed nor lives
been lived or lost. I did not stop
for long but still the line runs on:
Yes, I remember Adlestrop.

STELLA COWMEADOW

Blackbird of Arras

Yes, I will remember Adlestrop –
that name, for the slipping time
left today. The blackbird singing,
as it did then, a fluting chime,

upon the bleak trenches edge,
this road now taken, its warning
unheeded. One day halting
in June heat, willow-herb adorning,

the platform silent. Here the sky puffs
in loud smoke, haycocks mound
from stricken earth. Oh, Gloucestershire,
oh, Oxfordshire, rejoice in the sound

of blackbird's bewitching chorus.
In a moment's respite I stand and stare
to see the creature wildly flap away
and feel the sudden rush of air.

Tony Vincent Isaacs

Easter Monday, 1917, Arras, Pas-de-Calais. Edward Thomas,
poet, killed by shell blast.

Remembering 'Adlestrop'

I do remember 'Adlestrop';
Recited to me on the tow-path
That day we walked the Cherwell
To where it meets the Oxford cut.

I teased you to quote me a poem;
You cleared your throat in mock drama
And spoke perfection as river
And canal waltzed their lazy routes.

Sitting against the wall of the
Derelict cement factory you
Told me of the blast that stopped
His heart, his body left unmarked.

And that's when I saw what Thomas saw;
In the cow parsley and in the songs
And swoops of Oxfordshire's birds,
I understood 'Adlestrop'.

BOB HILL

Someone cleared his throat…

Oh sorry, that was me! I didn't think you'd hear me.
But are you pleased at how much still remains?
You look around, and nothing much has altered –
You had your cars, your telephones, your planes.

There must be something new that will impress you.
Look at this gadget – that's my mobile phone!
I can do emails, google, surf the ether!
You smile and ask where all the flowers have gone?

'But this is all?' you murmur. 'This is nothing!
A thousand flowers bloomed here. These few remain?
Where are the birds, the insects' drowsy humming?'
You shake your head and get back on your train.

I'm glad you don't know where that train is heading
Towards your flimsy dugout on the Somme
Blocking your ears against the martial thunder
Then blown to bloody ruin by a bomb.

RICHARD VAUGHAN-DAVIES

My Dear Cassandra

Yes, I remember Adlestrop
As it was before Repton came.
Now the Pleasure Grounds are improved.
– The Village may not think the same.

James-Henry showed us the Prospect,
– Far and farther. All the Birds yet
Of Oxfordshire and Gloucestershire
Talked more sense than the Pump Room Set.

On Friday we dine at Daylesford.
What a happy Party will meet!
– I shall wear my new grass green Gown,
& perk my Cap with Meadowsweet.

We worshipped in the handsome Church,
Glad of shade on the hot June day,
– & that feeling of peacefulness.
      Yours affectionately, J.A.

Celia Jones

Journey (after Edward Thomas)

Some years after hearing your poem read
At school as I gazed out the window, (poem unheard),
My mind mistier and mistier
Bored of all your unknown haycocks and willow-herb,
I took a steam train, the tourist line,
Too young to call this recall or memory,
Newly found interest in what to me was history
Alone on the platform I stood, blue sky above
Listening to the train's shriek and gun like rattle,
And in that moment mind cleared and I thought of family,
Those now gone and those yet to come.
Then in summer heat the train pulled away, left me,
Clearing my throat, struggling for words,
Distance growing farther and farther
Only then I understood and strained to hear the birds
Of all Oxfordshire and Gloucestershire.

RIFF POYNTON

Tackley Halt 26th August 1970

Oh, I remember Tackley Halt,
the name, because one August day,
at dawn, a goods train was derailed there
violently: one wagon on its side,

sleepers cracked, the down-line twisted up,
a platform ripped apart; leaning on the gate
three village boys, curious, had come to see
the tumbled trucks, the splintered station name.

And nearby, fields of mugwort, wild
Angelica and rootless scabious
were hedged with drooping elder fruit,
tangled in bramble and old man's beard.

There, throughout the cloudless day,
a grasshopper warbler, from its hidden nest
in tussocks of late summer grass,
sang out its high, rhythmic, chirring note.

HILDA REED

Uncle Dick

It was always a world away – Adlestrop.
But the old man was real.
Cord-breeched, white-whiskered, breathing harsh,
In his cottage on the bank.

Tiny windows, oak settle,
Strong tea, bread and yellow butter,
Beetroot and spice of spring onions
From the garden tumbled with nasturtiums and roses.

'He had a hard life', said my aunt.
His father died worn out.
And so did he, ag lab in pretty Adlestrop,
While his brothers laid the lines he never travelled on.

The birds still sing in leafy Gloucestershire
For phantom listeners on the vanished platform.
The trains still pass and bear the people off
To offices in cities worlds away.

Pamela Hawker

'Uncle Dick' was real. He was Richard Barnes 1861-1946. All the details are
true, I met him as a child, only once.

By Heart

Yes I remember 'Adlestrop',
the pain – forced to learn by rote and
perform under Mr Martin's
sneering watch; embarrassment not

unwonted (which I'd had to look
up in the Dictionary), and
how the class returned his smirk as
my hand was first again when asked

what a haycock was, being a
Country Girl (or at least from the
ru-urban fringes), and how for
that minute I closed my eyes and

could see it all, wished I could be
there in hazed sun and shire birdsong;
anywhere but that room; dying.
Someone cleared their throat. The spell broke.

KATE WISE

Going to Adlestrop

On the green, the platform's name board,
in the shop, your words in pencil. I'm told:
Twenty minutes to the line. No mention
of the ghost station, only the mud-laden field.

Walking back, I saw hollyhocks bold
as bugles flanking every door I passed,
thought of you: all the years of suffering
and how you found your voice at last,

how soon lost it. I felt like kneeling
by the stone cottages and weeping
but a swallow twittered into eaves,
from a tree came the sound of cheeping,

on a hill I glimpsed haymaking.
Suddenly in the haze you were there
and I seemed to hear all the birds
singing in Oxford and Gloucestershire.

Myra Schneider

Titlestrop

No, he did not remember *Titlestrop.*
That sign did not come into view
On Midsummer's day '14 – and if it had
Would Teddy Thomas have worked

A pastoral gem with Adlestrop's
Former name? Or instead had thoughts
Of a stamping, angry poet's block;
An elusive search for the perfect frame

For still cloudlets high in his Cotswold sky –
As steam hissed, a blackbird sang, haycocks dried.
Would he have just passed on by, cleared
His throat and wondered why

The bare, unwonted platform bore
Such a stroppy sign, not stopped to share
The sounds of all the misty, far-flung birds
Of Gloucestershire and Oxfordshire?

JILL MUNRO

Edward Thomas at Gidea Park

You are amongst the legions,
men in khaki, waiting on the platform.
They are all young and you are pleased
to be caught up in their urgency.

On the same platform, there's a younger officer
named Owen, with a different company.
You'll never meet. Except, perhaps, on this occasion –
getting your men onto the train.

You brush past, apologise, for getting in his way,
then climb into the crowded carriage.
Something snags at your attention
like a bobby's button caught on a sleeve.

You glance back, notice Owen's raised hand
his fingers stained with ink,
but the guard blows his whistle
and your train pulls away.

Caroline M. Davies

It seems likely that two of the finest poets of the war may have seen
each other or even spoken, before going about their army business
none the wiser.

Matthew Hollis – *Now All Roads lead to France.*

Reading Adlestrop

Two tourists stand at the shelter,
she says to him Look, there's a poem.
The noise of passing juggernauts
makes him ask What? What did you say?
She points, On this plaque, four little verses.
Hesitating she begins to read,
he fishes for his glasses and joins in.

Puzzled at first by all that's unfamiliar,
words reel them in, peel away the present,
their travelling jumble of Cotswold cottages,
Oxford colleges, birthplace half-timbering,
until they sit with Edward Thomas
in that summer's heat and stillness.
Like him they are innocent of knowledge.

No mud and mortars cloud the poem.
Traffic passes and close by a blackbird sings.

PAMELI BENHAM

Well was it all worth it? The meetings, emails, telephone calls, changes of plans, last minute doubts and uncertainties? There was no permanent reminder of the event after all.

The answer is an unqualified YES! The whole day was a tremendous success, and we in Cotswold Line Promotion Group are honoured and proud to have worked with the Adlestrop community to deliver the commemorative train ride for the centenary day. It is difficult now to remember where the idea of a train started – suffice to say that everyone involved was fully committed throughout the planning of it. Many of us would have liked to repeat the full steam operation of the original train. That was not to be, as the main purpose – to replicate the actual centenary day and time – was the right decision, and that meant a Tuesday rather than a weekend when a steam operation might have been possible.

So everything about the train went to plan. The day was fine, including the requisite 'cloudlets'. The train was well loaded, but not uncomfortably full. There were period costumes and picnic baskets, and we all shared the sense of being part of a very special event. The train stopped, not at the site of the former station, but at a point in full view of the terrace of Adlestrop House, and the reading of the poem was made over the train's public address system by CLPG President Lord Faulkner of Worcester, followed by a recording of blackbird song. And in the adjacent field there appeared a choir, apparently singing. But because we did not know in advance that they would be there we could not switch off the train engines and hear them!

The aftermath has been a permanent memory for all involved, and the creation of a surplus which will be shared between ourselves and the Adlestrop community. We must all be grateful to First Great Western who worked so hard with us to make all of the arrangements, and who donated their share of the surplus from the train income to the memorial fund for our founding Chairman, Oliver Lovell. Oliver would have been delighted with the day.

So we hope to have been able to present the cheque for the surplus to the village at the launch of this book, and to further demonstrate that it was all worth it!

John Ellis
Chairman
Cotswold Line Promotion Group

Index of poets

Index of first lines

ADLESTROP